PRACTISE & PASS 11+
ENGLISH
PRACTICE PAPERS

Contents

- Practice paper 1 — 3
- Practice paper 2 — 15
- Practice paper 3 — 27
- Practice paper 4 — 39
- Writing — 51

© Peter Williams and Trotman Publishing, 2015

The right of Peter Williams to be identified as the author of this work has been asserted by him in accordance with the Copyright, Designs and Patents Act, 1988.

All rights reserved. No part of this publication may be transmitted in any form or by any means, or stored in a retrieval system without prior written permission from the publisher.

First published 2015 by Trotman Publishing, a division of Crimson Publishing Ltd, 19–21c Charles Street, Bath BA1 1HX.

ISBN 978 1 84455 427 0

A catalogue record for this book is available from the British Library.

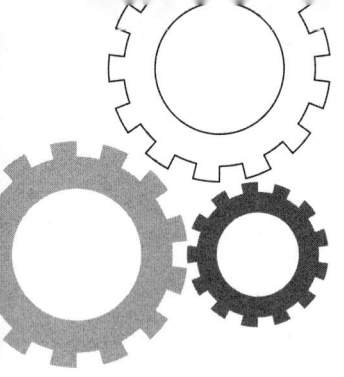

PRACTISE & PASS 11+

ENGLISH
MULTIPLE CHOICE

PRACTICE PAPER 1

Read the following instructions carefully.

1. Do <u>not</u> begin until you are told to do so.
2. This is a multiple choice test.
3. Answers should be marked on the answer sheet provided.
4. Mark your answer in the same number on the answer sheet as the test question by drawing a firm line clearly through the rectangle next to your answer.
5. If you make a mistake, make sure you rub it out completely before putting a new answer in. There should be only one answer marked for each question.
6. You may do any working out on a separate sheet of paper.
7. Make sure you keep your place on the answer sheet.
8. You will have 50 minutes to complete this test.
9. Work quickly and carefully. If you cannot do a question, do not waste time on it but move on to the next. If you are unsure of the answer, choose the one that you think is best.

Read the passage below carefully and answer the questions that follow.

Waterways of the World – by P.J. Williams

Stretching for hundreds of miles and linking some of the most important and busiest seas of the world, the largest of the world's canals provide quicker access routes for global shipping. Others provide vital routes for transporting cargoes of all types in and out of major ports and cities around the world.

5   But it wasn't always this way – for many years fearless sailors sailed the world's seas in search of trading partners, new, diverse foods, cloth and other items. The dangers they faced, however, were many and, quite often, deadly. Furious, raging storms can cause a shipwreck – the ship can be thrown upon rocks, battered and ripped apart by monstrous winds and rains or pushed far off course by powerful currents.

10 Some of the most feared waters for sailors were around the southern tip of the Cape of Good Hope (located in South Africa), and also Cape Horn (located in South America); the waters which flowed past both of these headlands have been responsible for the fate of many a ship and its occupants. In addition, the distances that ships had to cover in order to travel around these dangerous capes were vast. It meant that ships could be at sea for many weeks or even months,
15 and goods could be spoiled, lost or stolen during that time. Something needed to be done to make shipping and trading safer and faster.

The Panama Canal

As far back as the sixteenth century, explorers had begun to look for a shorter route between the Pacific and Atlantic Oceans near the Americas. Several ideas were proposed, including a canal through either Nicaragua or Panama. These two countries were targeted for differing reasons. Panama was preferred
20 since its narrow isthmus between the Pacific and Atlantic Oceans meant less land to excavate. Although Charles V of Spain commissioned designers and architects to draw up plans for such a canal, no action was taken and it was some 350 years later that interest was once more renewed in the scheme.

In the latter part of the nineteenth century, it seemed that the scheme would be possible and after several treaties and agreements between the United States of America and Panama, work
25 was finally able to begin. It took some ten years to build – ostensibly by the United States Army Corps of Engineers – and the first ships passed through its 80-kilometre length in 1914. When the Panama Canal was constructed, engineers agreed that it would be best to create several sets of double lock gates since the canal runs into several lakes and these are not all at the same level. The Gatun Locks – three in all – raise ships just over 25 metres. From here the mighty vessels
30 pass through the Gatun Lake and into the Gaillard Cut. They then enter the Pedro Miguel Lock, which lowers them about 9 metres. But that isn't the end of it as the ships then pass through

the Miraflores Lake before entering a final set of two locks, which lower the ships the remaining 16 metres to the level of the Pacific Ocean. It is little wonder, then, that the Panama Canal is renowned for being an amazing feat of engineering.

35 The engineers faced another problem too – before the digging even commenced! The area through which the canal was to pass was a haven for mosquitoes – the insect responsible for carrying the deadly affliction malaria. Before the sappers could begin their work, the Medical Corps of the US Army had to spend valuable time and resources trying to eliminate the plagues of mosquitoes that frequented the area so that work could continue without delay.

40 It's been calculated that the canal shortens the distance for shipping by up to 14,000 kilometres on some routes. More than 12,000 ships pass through it annually. It now takes ships about seven or eight hours to cross from one ocean to the other and eliminates the danger of sailing around Cape Horn.

The Suez Canal

Like its little brother in Panama, the concept of building a link between the Mediterranean Sea and the Red Sea was conceived long before the canal was finally constructed. As far back as the
45 thirteenth century BC, a canal was first excavated – possibly under the rule of Ramses II of Egypt. However, the canal was not maintained and began to silt up, despite some efforts to keep it running. It was abandoned in the 8th century AD.

In a similar way to the Panama Canal, the idea of excavating was talked about for many years without action, until 1859 when digging began once more in earnest. The canal was opened in
50 1869 and is now about 195 kilometres in length. Also like the Panama Canal, it can accommodate huge vessels – yet there is a major difference between these two important waterways.

Since the levels of the Red Sea and the Mediterranean Sea are the same, there was no need to build locks in the Suez Canal, despite the fact that it is some three times the length of the Panama Canal. Undoubtedly this means that valuable time is saved as vessels passing through Suez need
55 not wait for locks to raise and lower gargantuan ships.

There is, however, something that does slow the pace of ships passing through the Suez Canal – and that is the fact that there is only one lane through which ships can pass. So how do these mighty metal containers cope when they approach one another? The designers of the canal decided to create extra passing lanes at various strategic points in the canal. In this way ships can
60 pull into these areas and wait while another ship passes them in the main canal. The Panama Canal needs no such passing lanes as its designers spent extra time and money ensuring that it was wide enough for two ships to pass from the outset.

The Manchester Ship Canal

The Manchester Ship Canal, unlike the two canals mentioned above, does not link two expanses of water via a canal. Instead it provides a vital artery into the heart of Manchester from the port of

65 Liverpool. The canal starts at the River Mersey estuary and runs some 58 kilometres north-east to Salford Quays.

It is similar to the Panama Canal in that it too has several sets of locks, including the largest set in England measuring 180 metres in length and 24 metres in width. The canal was built because there were few ways to transport goods from the north-west of England – the main one being
70 via railway, which was becoming too expensive. It was thought that the major industries of wool, glass, pottery and coal would benefit greatly by creating a vital link to the port of Liverpool in order to ship these goods to other parts of the country.

The canal also flows beneath the world's first and only swing aqueduct, which was designed to carry the Bridgewater Canal above the Manchester Ship Canal and is still in full working order
75 today. Like the Suez Canal, Manchester's Ship Canal was built in the nineteenth century and was opened in 1894. Unlike the Suez and Panama Canals, this gentle giant no longer boasts the volume of traffic it once did and is now used more by pleasure boats than ocean-going ships. Beautiful narrow boats chug lazily along the waterway while their passengers discover new wonders along the way.

What next?

80 Although these canals were built over a century ago, there can be little doubt that they have helped to improve global shipping by shortening many popular trade routes. They also make them safer by bypassing some of the more dangerous areas that sailors had to navigate in the past. Canals that bore into the heart of countries continue to provide vital transportation routes so goods can be delivered and exported in larger loads.

85 Will canals continue to be used long into the next century? No one can say for sure but it is likely that they will continue to serve a vital purpose for as long as there is major shipping between countries.

And while some canals might lose their traffic, they may well retain their charm and the stories associated with their history.

Now answer these questions (look at the passage again if you need to). You should choose the best answer and mark its letter on your answer sheet.

1 Which is the longest of the canals mentioned?

   A   Panama Canal
   B   Salford Quays
   C   Manchester Ship Canal
   D   Suez Canal
   E   Bridgewater Canal

2 Which two bodies of water does the Suez Canal link?

   A   Atlantic and Pacific Oceans
   B   Mediterranean Sea and Pacific Ocean
   C   Mediterranean Sea and Atlantic Ocean
   D   Red Sea and Pacific Ocean
   E   Red Sea and Mediterranean Sea

3 Why was the Panama Canal built with a series of locks?

   A   So the canal could be closed each night.
   B   So ships could pass each other in the canal.
   C   Because the two seas it linked were at different heights.
   D   To prevent flooding in the local area.
   E   To slow ships down when passing through the canal.

4 Why does the author refer to the Panama Canal as the Suez Canal's 'little brother'? (line 43)

   A   They were designed by the same people.
   B   The designer of the Suez Canal was the older brother of the designer of the Panama Canal.
   C   The Suez Canal is older and larger than the Panama Canal.
   D   The Panama Canal didn't take as long to build.
   E   Canals around the world are seen as being members of the same family.

Go straight on to the next page

5 Apart from the canal's construction, what other difficulty did engineers at Panama have to overcome?

- A They had to get rid of swarms of mosquitoes.
- B They had to persuade the people of Panama that they needed a canal.
- C They had to cut through really hard rock.
- D They had to employ many people to do the work.
- E They could only dig when there were no storms.

6 How many locks does the Suez Canal have?

- A 0
- B 1
- C 2
- D 3
- E 4

7 What feature of the Suez Canal may cause delays for ships using the canal?

- A It is extremely long.
- B It is mostly uphill.
- C It has many sharp bends.
- D It has only one lane for ships with passing points.
- E It has an extremely slow speed limit for ships.

8 Why did industrialists deem it necessary to build the Manchester Ship Canal?

- A The roads were not very good.
- B The railways had become too expensive.
- C Canals were the safest form of transport.
- D People liked using canals as they were picturesque.
- E The Manchester Ship Canal had several locks.

Go straight on to the next page

9 Apart from being a safer route, what other advantage did using the Panama Canal have for traders?

- A It significantly reduced the distance ships had to travel.
- B It meant sailors could have more time off.
- C It meant that ships could be more heavily loaded.
- D It meant sailors were more likely to catch malaria.
- E It meant ships could travel at faster speeds.

10 What evidence is there that the Panama Canal was first devised in the sixteenth century?

- A Traders have always wanted a safer and shorter route.
- B Charles V of Spain commissioned architects to look into it.
- C Ramses II first came up with the idea.
- D The US Army Corps had always wanted to build a canal there.
- E Pedro Miguel first thought of the idea.

11 Approximately how long does it take a ship to travel from the Pacific Ocean to the Atlantic Ocean using the Panama Canal?

- A 1 day
- B 6 to 7 days
- C 1 month
- D 1 hour
- E 7 to 8 hours

12 Why is the Panama Canal 'renowned for being an amazing feat of engineering'?

- A It is extremely long.
- B There were many obstacles making it hard to build.
- C It is able to raise and lower huge ships using several locks.
- D It shortens the distance between the Pacific and Atlantic Oceans.
- E It is a route across an entire country.

Go straight on to the next page

13 Another appropriate title for this piece of writing could have been:

- A Getting more vehicles off the roads
- B Cruising around the world
- C Global man-made water links
- D Sailing the seven seas
- E Building dams and lakes

Now answer these questions about the meanings of words and how they are used in the passage.

14 'isthmus' (line 20) refers to . . .

- A two seas joined by a canal
- B a long, narrow strip of water
- C a large island
- D a bridge over a canal
- E a narrow strip of land between two seas

15 'excavated' (line 45) means . . .

- A constructed
- B dug out
- C filled with water
- D designed
- E created

16 Another word for 'vessels' (line 54) could be . . .

- A canal
- B ship
- C bridge
- D lock gate
- E river

17 Another word for 'navigate' (line 82) could be . . .

    A   transport
    B   trade
    C   enjoy
    D   worry
    E   negotiate

Now answer these questions about what kinds of words are used in the passage.

18 'mighty metal' (line 58) is an example of . . .

    A   hyperbole
    B   alliteration
    C   simile
    D   onomatopoeia
    E   metaphor

19 'gargantuan' (line 55) is what part of speech?

    A   conjunction
    B   noun
    C   preposition
    D   adjective
    E   adverb

20 'purpose' (line 86) is what type of word?

    A   proper noun
    B   pronoun
    C   concrete noun
    D   abstract noun
    E   common noun

Go straight on to the next page

In the passage below there are some spelling mistakes. On each line there is either one mistake or no mistake. Find the group of words with the mistake in it and mark its letter on your answer sheet. If there is no mistake, mark 'E' on your answer sheet.

The Police Report

21 The weather was dull and gloomey when I arrived — None
   A · B · C · D — E

22 at the sceen of the alleged crime. Looking around I — None
   A · B · C · D — E

23 quickly established that the culprit had escaped on — None
   A · B · C · D — E

24 foot, so I decided to give chase. As I was preceeding — None
   A · B · C · D — E

25 in a westerley direction along King Street, I noticed — None
   A · B · C · D — E

26 a peculiar looking trail which dissapeared beneath — None
   A · B · C · D — E

27 a pair of gigantic steel doors. I felt suspitious so that — None
   A · B · C · D — E

28 was when I felt it necessary to telephone for extra help. — None
   A · B · C · D — E

29 However, when my colleages arrived, we were too late — None
   A · B · C · D — E

30 to apprahend the suspects. The building was deserted. — None
   A · B · C · D — E

Go straight on to the next page

In the passage below there are some punctuation mistakes. On each line there is either one mistake or no mistake. Find the group of words with the mistake in it and mark its letter on your answer sheet. If there is no mistake, mark 'E' on your answer sheet.

In the Mountains

31. Ralph stared down at / his friend penny / as she / carefully / None
    A / B / C / D / E

32. levered herself / closer to / his ledge Using / strategically / None
    A / B / C / D / E

33. placed handhold's, / she made / steady / progress and / None
    A / B / C / D / E

34. finally reached / her friend. / As they sat / high up on the / None
    A / B / C / D / E

35. side of / the mountain, / they admired / the amazing view? / None
    A / B / C / D / E

36. 'Isnt it wonderful?' / breathed Penny, / and she / turned to / None
    A / B / C / D / E

37. her friend. / Awesome,' replied / Ralph / as he gazed across / None
    A / B / C / D / E

38. at the farms, / forests, / rivers, and countryside / which lay / None
    A / B / C / D / E

39. sprawled out / before them. / 'Shall we climb / even higher? / None
    A / B / C / D / E

40. he asked / Penny, / and she nodded / enthusiastically. / None
    A / B / C / D / E

In each of the questions below you have to choose the best word or group of words to complete the passage so that it makes sense and uses correct, standard English. Choose one of the five answers each time and mark its letter on the answer sheet.

A Difficult Voyage

41 The tiny boat rocked and [pitted A] [pitched B] [patted C] [put D] [pulled E] as the

42 ocean unleashed its full [furey A] [furry B] [ferry C] [fury D] [firey E] in the form of

43 a [topical A] [tropical B] [typical C] [total D] [troubled E] storm. The captain and his

44 three stalwart [passengers A] [passages B] [passers C] [pacers D] [pagers E] gripped

45 the sides of the [hurl A] [hole B] [whole C] [herl D] [hull E] to avoid being thrown

46 overboard. The little boat [cracked A] [crocked B] [croaked C] [crekt D] [creaked E]

47 in protest as waves [crasht A] [crashing B] [crash C] [crashed D] [crushed E] over the

48 wooden sides of the [vassal A] [vessel B] [vesell C] [vassal D] [vassall E]. After many

49 hours the storm [abated A] [bated B] [beated C] [boated D] [abating E] and the brave

50 [travelling A] [travelers B] [travellers C] [trawlers D] [travels E] were finally safe.

END OF TEST – PLEASE CHECK ALL YOUR ANSWERS

PRACTISE & PASS 11+

ENGLISH
MULTIPLE CHOICE

PRACTICE PAPER 2

Read the following instructions carefully.

1. Do not begin until you are told to do so.
2. This is a multiple choice test.
3. Answers should be marked on the answer sheet provided.
4. Mark your answer in the same number on the answer sheet as the test question by drawing a firm line clearly through the rectangle next to your answer.
5. If you make a mistake, make sure you rub it out completely before putting a new answer in. There should be only one answer marked for each question.
6. You may do any working out on a separate sheet of paper.
7. Make sure you keep your place on the answer sheet.
8. You will have 50 minutes to complete this test.
9. Work quickly and carefully. If you cannot do a question, do not waste time on it but move on to the next. If you are unsure of the answer, choose the one that you think is best.

Read the passage below carefully and answer the questions that follow.

Behind the Bookcase – by P.J. Williams

Octavia stalked stealthily along the edge of the room. Here the floorboards were bare but pitted with groove-like marks where some sort of heavy object had once passed, its ferocious teeth grinding into the unprotected wood.

Her objective? The bookcase. It stood tall as a mountain with a mass of ledges of various shapes and sizes jutting out, none of which appeared to follow any particular order. It was her favourite place to be, set as it was in one corner of the room and covered by a soft blanket of shade. Here she could lose herself and hide away from the rest of the world.

She tiptoed carefully towards it, always taking care that she should not be seen. After all, she would not want to disturb the 'watchers'. Those self-appointed guardians of the 'books' with their colossal and cumbersome forms would stop at nothing to drive her from this place so she approached with a combination of caution and alertness.

As she entered the kingdom of shadow, she felt she could breathe more easily – there had been no evidence of any watchers nearby and she was at the first of the shelves. She relaxed. Good. A dark, sinister form with a bright hourglass shape painted across its middle dropped down just beside her! 'Boo!' Octavia sprang back with a scream and dashed for the nearest gap she could find. Behind her she heard the sound of high-pitched laughter, but although she thought she recognised it, it was only when she was safely hidden that she risked a furtive glance around the corner to see who her would-be assailant was.

Amelia! Octavia trotted from her sanctuary, casting her eyes towards the floor as she approached her friend. There was little point in pretending she hadn't been frightened by Amelia's prank – it was clear she had been scared out of her wits!

Amelia grinned mischievously and rasped, 'So how are we today little Octavia? Surely you didn't think that I was a watcher?'

Octavia forced a smile back. 'Some friend you are,' she blurted out. 'Haven't you got better things to do than jumping out on your friends?'

'I could always have bitten you,' Amelia suggested. This time her broad grin revealed a pair of fearsome fangs, which had only one deadly use. Octavia suppressed a shudder. 'Hmmm, I suppose I should be glad that we are friends then – and that I would not make much of a meal.' She tried to sound cool, but there was no mistaking that she had more than a healthy respect for her companion. They both knew that one bite from Amelia's teeth would prove fatal, as they were soaked in lethal venom. Even the watchers feared Amelia – another reason why they would be so keen to get rid of both of them should they discover their hiding place.

Amelia knew she had made her point, but did not delight in Octavia's discomfort so suggested they continue their journey together and creep behind the bookcase. The bookcase was freestanding, and where its foundations met the skirting board, a large gap was created – easily spacious enough for the two friends to fit through. Octavia agreed uncertainly, but soon began to relax once more as Amelia disclosed that she had found a hidden room under the bottom shelf and that they should explore it together.

'Who made it?' asked Octavia, who, curious by nature, was filled with questions. 'Is it safe? I mean, have you actually been inside it yet or have you only just discovered it?'

'All in good time,' Amelia chuckled, 'All in good . . .'

She raised an arm and put it across Octavia's chest, holding her back. Simultaneously she crouched low to the ground, tensing her muscles. Sensing the unseen danger, Octavia assumed the same pose and whispered hoarsely, 'What is it? What do you see?'

Amelia signalled with another arm, and Octavia followed the direction of her point. She inhaled sharply as she now saw it too. Looming large on the wall across the room was an enormous shadow. Moving menacingly and silently like an ominous cloud in an overcast sky, it enveloped increasingly more of the wall as it approached them.

'Has it seen us?' gasped Octavia.
'I'm not sure.'
'Should we stay put or make a break for it?'
'It's hard to tell.'

The shadow was creeping ever closer. Octavia was not afraid to say that she was terrified, yet she trusted Amelia who had survived more dealings with watchers than many of their kind.

Then it stopped. Inexplicably it stopped. Octavia began to relax once more.

'Get ready,' murmured her friend. 'When I say, we dash behind the shelf.'

Rotating slowly, the shadow's shape transformed from an incongruous blob to something with five clear arms. The end of each arm was sharp, rounded, and hardened. Each end was also a bright scarlet colour and one of the arms had a gleaming band of metal surrounding it. It paused for what seemed like an eternity . . .

'Now!' yelled Amelia, and she sprinted across the final part of open ground. As though hit by a bolt of lightning, Octavia hurtled after her, not daring to look at the umbrous form above them, which, even as they sped, had begun its downward death-dealing blow.

Whump! Behind them a massive fleshy form crashed from the sky, missing them by a hair as they dashed to safety. The air seemed to be trapped then a powerful gust washed over them, nearly causing them to tumble from their feet. Indeed it would have done so had they not secured themselves with their suction pads first.

'Wha-what was that?' stammered Octavia when she could finally get the words out.

'That, my friend,' answered Amelia, 'was the attack of a watcher. They know we are faster so they try to creep up, then pause, then attack, hoping we haven't noticed them. And that is why we must always be mindful of shadows on the wall.'

Yet, even as she spoke these words of advice to her friend, a booming growl resounded around the room. 'I'll get you, you little pest!' it declared.

Suddenly books started crashing from the bookshelf. Some, which hadn't seen the light of day for many years, tumbled haphazardly from their resting places, crashing upon the floor. Others seemed to fly, nearly crashing against the wall on the opposite side of the room.

Without a moment's thought Amelia grabbed Octavia's arm and dragged her from their hiding place down to a crevice beneath the very structure of the bookcase itself. She pulled her through the tiny opening and thence to another in the floorboards. They climbed down into the darkness and listened to the clamour above.

'What's going on?' wailed a petrified Octavia.
'They want me,' stated Amelia quietly. 'They've been hunting me for several days now. They fear me for what I can do . . .' her voice trailed off.
Octavia gulped, 'Thank you, Amelia. You saved . . .'
'Your life? No – I shouldn't have put you in danger. They don't mind you so much; you don't pose any threat.'

There was bitterness in her voice, and Octavia felt a pang of pity for her friend. She pondered the irony of the fact that what made Amelia so dangerous to others also put her own life in danger.

They listened to the thunder above their heads of more blameless books clattering from the bookcase shelves.

'Listen,' said Amelia when the rumbling finally ceased. Her eyes glistened in a thin shaft of light that shone through a tiny nook in the boards. 'I don't think we should meet up any more. They want me too badly and they won't stop hunting until they either catch me, or . . .'
'Or what?'
'Or I leave.'
'Perhaps it's best if you do then,' ventured Octavia. 'But if you do I'll be coming with you. If that's all right with you?'

Octavia was sure she noticed a brief smile cross Amelia's face as she responded, 'Thank you – I'd like that.'

Now answer these questions (look at the passage again if you need to). You should choose the best answer and mark its letter on your answer sheet.

1 Why did Octavia like the bookcase?

- A   She loved to read.
- B   She met her friend Amelia there.
- C   It was a safe place to be alone.
- D   It was nice to be in the shade.
- E   She could see the 'watchers' from it.

2 What did Octavia think was attacking her in paragraph 4?

- A   Amelia
- B   a sinister shadow
- C   a watcher
- D   an hourglass
- E   the bookcase

3 What made Amelia so dangerous?

- A   She had sharp fangs.
- B   She was good at jumping out at others.
- C   She was bigger than her friends.
- D   Even the watchers were afraid of her.
- E   She injected poison when she bit.

4 In paragraph 2 what do you think the author means by 'a mass of ledges'?

- A   different sized books
- B   the book shelves
- C   rocky ledges
- D   skirting boards
- E   wooden floorboards

Go straight on to the next page

5 How did Amelia know a 'watcher' was approaching?

- A Books were tumbled from the bookcase.
- B She could hear the approach of their feet.
- C She saw a large fleshy five-armed creature.
- D She noticed a shadow moving on the wall.
- E She noticed something behind the bookcase.

6 What did Amelia say she had discovered behind the bookcase?

- A a rare book
- B a secret passage
- C a watcher
- D a skirting board
- E a secret room

7 Where did the two friends hide while the books were thrown from the bookcase?

- A low, against the floor
- B under the floorboards
- C in a secret passage
- D behind the skirting board
- E in a crevice in the wall

8 Why did the watchers want to get rid of Amelia so much?

- A She was often scaring people.
- B She didn't like the watchers.
- C She could hurt them with her venomous bite.
- D They disliked her friend Octavia.
- E They disliked her messing up the books.

Go straight on to the next page

9 What action does Amelia suggest that shows she cares for Octavia?

- A They hide until the watcher leaves.
- B She and Octavia leave that place forever.
- C She and Octavia do not meet any more.
- D She should not visit the bookcase any more.
- E Octavia should not visit the bookcase any more.

10 'Some, which hadn't seen the light of day for many years . . .' – what does this description tell you about some of the books?

- A Those books were new to the bookcase.
- B Those books were only read in dark places.
- C Those books were written about the night.
- D Those books were only read during the day.
- E Those books had not been read for a long time.

11 Why do the watchers have to creep up on Amelia and Octavia?

- A Because usually they make too much noise and are heard.
- B Because they are slower and have to get close before they attack.
- C Because they are cowardly and won't attack them face-to-face.
- D Because they live in the bookcase.
- E Because they need to turn around before they attack.

12 What was the 'incongruous blob'?

- A a flying weapon
- B a monster
- C a hand
- D the arms of a watcher
- E the tentacles of a watcher

13 'There was bitterness in her voice . . .' – why does Amelia feel envious of Octavia?

- A She thinks Octavia has more friends so the 'watchers' don't chase her.
- B She feels Octavia is more attractive so she is liked more.
- C She resents the fact that as Octavia is not poisonous she is not hunted.
- D She wishes she was as small as Octavia so she would not be seen by the 'watchers'.
- E She is envious because Octavia is more curious than her.

Now answer these questions about the meanings of words and how they are used in the passage.

14 'sanctuary' (line 19) refers to . . .

- A a secret place
- B a home
- C a place of safety
- D a dark place
- E a place near a bookcase

15 'like an ominous cloud in an overcast sky' (line 47) means . . .

- A It was about to rain heavily.
- B The shadow on the wall warned of danger.
- C The shadow was moving towards the bookcase.
- D Night time was approaching fast.
- E A watcher was flying towards them.

16 Another word for 'inexplicably' (line 55) could be . . .

- A amazingly
- B eventually
- C unremarkably
- D peculiarly
- E inevitably

17 Another word for 'haphazardly' (line 75) could be . . .

- A precariously
- B dangerously
- C devastatingly
- D orderly
- E randomly

Now answer these questions about what kinds of words are used in the passage.

18 'As though hit by a bolt of lightning' (lines 61–62) is an example of . . .

- A personification
- B alliteration
- C simile
- D onomatopoeia
- E metaphor

19 'danger', 'pity', 'respect', 'nature' are what part of speech?

- A conjunction
- B noun
- C preposition
- D adjective
- E adverb

20 'Whump' (line 64) is an example of . . .

- A personification
- B alliteration
- C simile
- D onomatopoeia
- E metaphor

In the passage below there are some spelling mistakes. On each line there is either one mistake or no mistake. Find the group of words with the mistake in it and mark its letter on your answer sheet. If there is no mistake, mark 'E' on your answer sheet.

A Cold-Blooded Life

21. For many years the world's / reptiles / have / sufered the — None
    A / B / C / D — E

22. unenvyable / fate of being / shunned, feared / and even — None
    A / B / C / D — E

23. hunted / by humans who / seem not / able to comprehend — None
    A / B / C / D — E

24. how they / live. Indeed / their existence / is sumwhat — None
    A / B / C / D — E

25. remarkable / since these / fasinating animals / have no — None
    A / B / C / D — E

26. inturnal / way of / regulating their / body temperature. — None
    A / B / C / D — E

27. That is, / they are / cold-blooded. / This would explaine — None
    A / B / C / D — E

28. why the vast / majority of / the world's / reptiles thrive in — None
    A / B / C / D — E

29. warmer countries. / Durring / daylight they / can soak up — None
    A / B / C / D — E

30. the sun's / warmth, ready / to become / preditors at night! — None
    A / B / C / D — E

In the passage below there are some punctuation mistakes. On each line there is either one mistake or no mistake. Find the group of words with the mistake in it and mark its letter on your answer sheet. If there is no mistake, mark 'E' on your answer sheet.

At the Market

31. The traders' / at the market / arrived early / and began setting / None
    A / B / C / D / E

32. out their stalls. / Amir ran a shoe stall, / and clive ran / the fruit / None
    A / B / C / D / E

33. and vegetable stall. / They were / good friend's, / and would / None
    A / B / C / D / E

34. often chat / when there were / not many / customers to serve. / None
    A / B / C / D / E

35. 'How's your foot' / Amir called / across to Clive / as they / None
    A / B / C / D / E

36. unpacked their / wares one day / 'Not bad / but could be / None
    A / B / C / D / E

37. better, / responded Clive / in a slightly / gloomy voice. 'How / None
    A / B / C / D / E

38. did you hurt / it anyway?' / asked Amir. / 'i twisted it when / None
    A / B / C / D / E

39. getting out / of my van / the other day,' / replied Clive. 'It / None
    A / B / C / D / E

40. still really aches, / but I hope / it will be / better soon' / None
    A / B / C / D / E

In each of the questions below you have to choose the best word or group of words to complete the passage so that it makes sense and uses correct, standard English. Choose one of the five answers each time and mark its letter on the answer sheet.

In the Moonlight

41 The pirate [bullion]A [stallion]B [gallon]C [galleon]D [hoard]E slipped

42 silently into the [hiding]A [sheltered]B [danger]C [famous]D [mountainous]E

43 cove. The ship's [sales]A [sails]B [ropes]C [oars]D [sheets]E were folded and

44 stored below the [sea]A [cave]B [mast]C [cabin]D [deck]E. Then the captain

45 [barked]A [asked]B [left]C [thought]D [said]E out orders to his crew, telling them

46 to [free]A [weigh]B [hoist]C [gather]D [store]E anchor. With their ship safe

47 the pirates climbed [over]A [abored]B [aboard]C [across]D [down]E their rowing

48 boat and [heaped]A [heeled]B [hefted]C [heaved]D [hopped]E on the wooden oars.

49 Soon they were at the [plank]A [gang]B [jetty]C [rocks]D [tavern]E unloading their

50 ill-gotten [sails]A [contraband]B [oars]C [chains]D [gunpowder]E.

END OF TEST - PLEASE CHECK ALL YOUR ANSWERS

PRACTISE & PASS 11+

ENGLISH
MULTIPLE CHOICE

PRACTICE PAPER 3

Read the following instructions carefully.

1. Do <u>not</u> begin until you are told to do so.

2. This is a multiple choice test.

3. Answers should be marked on the answer sheet provided.

4. Mark your answer in the same number on the answer sheet as the test question by drawing a firm line clearly through the rectangle next to your answer.

5. If you make a mistake, make sure you rub it out completely before putting a new answer in. There should be only one answer marked for each question.

6. You may do any working out on a separate sheet of paper.

7. Make sure you keep your place on the answer sheet.

8. You will have 50 minutes to complete this test.

9. Work quickly and carefully. If you cannot do a question, do not waste time on it but move on to the next. If you are unsure of the answer, choose the one that you think is best.

Read the passage below carefully and answer the questions that follow.

A Remarkable Scientist – by P.J. Williams

Have you ever broken or suspected that you have broken a bone? Perhaps you know of a friend or relative who has suffered this misfortune and had to be taken to the hospital. Once there, before deciding what to do, doctors will often ask for their patient to have an X-ray of the suspected broken bone.

5   When we first come across X-rays as children, they seem almost magical in nature. They are, of course, incredible science being used very helpfully. So what are they and how do they work? X-rays are a type of radiation. Radiation is often a word we associate with nuclear power plants and terrible accidents but the truth is that tiny amounts of it are used when we X-ray an area of the body. Provided we don't have too many X-rays in our lifetime, they are harmless. We can't see
10 X-rays of course and in many ways they are like light. The difference is that light is absorbed by the skin on our bodies but X-rays have a higher frequency and pass through us. As they pass through our bodies they do so at differing rates, depending on what they pass through. This is the reason that the insides of our bodies can be seen on the X-ray images when they are held up to the light. The really dense material such as our bones appear to be white, while softer parts, such as organs
15 like the heart or the lungs, seem to be much darker.

If the radiologist – the person who is responsible for taking and interpreting the X-rays – can see a dark line between the white of a bone, this is often the tell-tale sign that a break or fracture has occurred.

So what did doctors do before the days of radiologists, when they were unable to see inside the
20 human body? Well, often it was a case of trial and error, feeling carefully and listening to how each patient reacted when parts of the body were manipulated by hand. Of course, this method could never be as accurate as current practices, but many physicians considered it the best way.

That was until Marie Curie, among other scientists, came up with several remarkable breakthroughs.

25 For it was Marie Curie who first initiated the use of X-ray machines for medical purposes. How she was able to accomplish this is explained below, along with some of her many other scientific achievements. As you will discover when you read on, she was a truly extraordinary scientist.

Initially working alongside her husband Pierre at his laboratory in France, it was Marie who realised that some elements gave off radiation.

30 After much work together the Curies discovered an element which they named polonium after Marie's country of origin (she was from Poland). They first noticed it in 1898 and noted that this

element had radioactive properties. Radiation itself had already been discovered by French physicist Henri Becquerel. However this proved to be just the beginning as later on in 1898 the two of them discovered radium – which they named after the word radioactivity as it was highly radioactive.

35 Marie found that it was the amount of this element that affected how much radiation it emitted and this paved the way for future discoveries and uses of radium. It was these initial discoveries which spurred Marie on to greater things.

The Curies realised at the turn of the nineteenth century that they would need vast amounts of 'pitchblende' – the substance in which radium was hidden. So it was that, in 1902, they managed
40 to isolate a tiny amount of radium chloride from a ton of pitchblende. The work involved was painstakingly difficult and at the time nobody knew the dangers of being exposed to radiation for long periods. This would adversely affect Marie later on in her life.

The Curies' work had not gone unnoticed and in 1903 they jointly received the Nobel Prize for Physics with Henri Becquerel. This was the first time ever that a woman had been awarded a Nobel
45 Prize. However, it was still another seven years before Marie – working alone – was able to isolate the element radium. Realising the importance of what she had achieved, she refused to patent the process. Had Curie obtained a patent it would have prevented other scientists from using her methods without her permission and she did not want this to hinder the research of others.

The following year, Curie received the Nobel Prize for Chemistry. She remains one of only two
50 people to have received the prize in two different fields, which is an incredible achievement. Once again, Curie made great use of her raised profile and was able to convince the French government to provide the funds for the foundation of a Radium Institute. It was completed in 1914.

Yet, despite her successes, sadness and disaster were often to visit Marie. She was only eight years old when she lost one of her sisters to typhus and she was only 11 when she lost her mother who
55 had been fighting tuberculosis for several years. Yet despite this she continued to work assiduously and maintain top marks in her classes at school. Later on, when they had received their first Nobel Prize, disaster struck as her husband Pierre slipped and fell into the road. His head was crushed by a horse-drawn carriage and he died. Once again, despite her grief, Marie continued to work diligently on the task that she had begun with Pierre.

60 Surprisingly, with all this scientific investigation into elements and radioactivity, it was only at the commencement of the First World War that Curie was able to develop a rudimentary X-ray machine to help those with injuries. In 1914, at the outbreak of war, she realised how her knowledge of radium and radioactivity could help. She had the brilliant idea of obtaining as much X-ray equipment as possible and mounting it on mobile units that could travel where they were
65 most needed. Although there were only 20 mobile units, she also organised 200 more stationary units to be situated in army field hospitals. These were the first to be used to correctly identify fragments of shrapnel buried in the flesh of soldiers fighting in the war. Again, she shared her knowledge by teaching British and American allies how this worked. By the end of 1918, it was estimated that one million soldiers had been assisted by Curie's invention.

70 Building on this success, this brilliant scientist went on to develop a way for the gas radon to be used to sterilise infected wounds.

Even after the war had ended, Curie continued to help several centres of research by raising funds through tours of the United States of America, among other countries. Throughout the 1920s she travelled quite extensively, even though she would have preferred to be conducting her own
75 research.

It was in the summer of 1934 that Marie Curie died from leukaemia, which she is thought to have contracted from her proximity to radium for so much of her life. To this day, all her scientific notes are kept in lead-lined boxes due to their radioactivity and can only be handled by those wearing protective suits. Curie was said to have carried radium about in test tubes in her pockets
80 and noted that it gave off a strange glow in the dark – not something that would be permitted in laboratories today!

This marvellous scientist's legacy lives on strongly today. The Marie Curie Foundation for Cancer Research was set up in 1948 and she is the only woman to be buried in the Panthéon on her own merits. Her contributions to science and medicine were extensive and far ahead of her time.

85 So next time you or somebody you know needs an X-ray or other treatment involving radiation, just remember the extraordinary woman who set us on this amazing path of discovery.

Now answer these questions (look at the passage again if you need to). You should choose the best answer and mark its letter on your answer sheet.

1 Who is responsible for taking X-rays of patients?

    A   Marie Curie
    B   a doctor
    C   a surgeon
    D   a radiologist
    E   Henri Becquerel

2 What nationality was Marie Curie?

    A   French
    B   British
    C   Polish
    D   American
    E   European

3 In which year did Marie Curie win the Nobel Prize for Chemistry?

    A   1903
    B   1907
    C   1910
    D   1911
    E   1914

4 Why didn't Marie Curie patent the process by which she could isolate radium?

    A   Henri Becquerel did it before her.
    B   She wanted to share it with her husband Pierre.
    C   It was too expensive to patent it.
    D   She didn't know what patenting was.
    E   She wanted all scientists to be able to use her knowledge.

Go straight on to the next page

5 To what useful purpose did Marie use her raised profile after winning her second Nobel Prize?

　　A　She went on a tour of the United States of America.
　　B　She went home to Poland for a rest.
　　C　She put X-ray machines on vehicles and made them mobile.
　　D　She convinced the French government to set up a Radium Institute.
　　E　She set up her own laboratory in France.

6 What major world event sparked the first use of X-rays for medical purposes?

　　A　the Nobel Prize for Physics
　　B　the First World War
　　C　the discovery of polonium
　　D　the discovery of leukaemia
　　E　the Second World War

7 What made Marie's academic success as a child particularly special?

　　A　Nobody helped her with her homework.
　　B　Her mother and sister died while she was still at school.
　　C　She could not afford the textbooks.
　　D　She had to work to pay for her schooling.
　　E　She found academic studies difficult to master.

8 Why was Marie compelled to finish her work on radium alone?

　　A　Her husband had been killed in an accident.
　　B　Pierre had other projects to work on.
　　C　The laboratory in France could only afford one scientist.
　　D　She wanted to win a Nobel Prize alone.
　　E　She didn't want anyone else to be affected by the radiation which was a side effect of her studies.

Go straight on to the next page

9 Which phrase best reflects how Marie would have felt about touring countries to raise money for research?

- A She enjoyed being away from her studies for short periods.
- B She felt that the French government should fund the research.
- C She knew her colleagues would continue the research while she was gone.
- D She knew it was important but longed to be conducting research.
- E She felt privileged to be travelling extensively.

10 'contracted from her proximity to radium' (line 77) – what does the author mean by this?

- A She enjoyed working with radium.
- B It was caused by being too close to radium.
- C She was the only one permitted to use radium.
- D She was only allowed to use small amounts of radium.
- E It was part of her job to handle radium.

11 Why did Marie take such a risk by carrying radioactive material around in her pockets?

- A She wanted to discover what effects radiation has on the human body.
- B She was too involved in her research to worry about it.
- C She thought a small amount would not cause any problems.
- D She was unaware of the dangers of radiation.
- E She didn't want anyone else to be harmed by it.

12 What are 'fragments of shrapnel' (line 67)?

- A bandages
- B pieces of radium
- C pieces of metal
- D broken bones
- E human organs

Go straight on to the next page

13 How did doctors try to treat wounds before the invention of X-ray?

    A   They felt with their hands and watched how their patients responded.
    B   They used painkillers before they operated.
    C   They looked carefully and bandaged where they thought the wound was.
    D   They let the wound heal on its own.
    E   They had to cut the wound open to see what was wrong.

Now answer these questions about the meanings of words and how they are used in the passage.

14 'manipulated' (line 21) means . . .

    A   moved by hand
    B   observed
    C   discovered
    D   treated
    E   injured

15 'and far ahead of her time' (line 84) means . . .

    A   Her work took a long time to complete.
    B   She didn't really understand what she was doing.
    C   Her ideas needed to catch up with the time in which she lived.
    D   Her ideas were very advanced for the time in which she lived.
    E   Other scientists had already had all of her ideas before.

16 Another word for 'legacy' (line 82) could be . . .

    A   heritage
    B   amazement
    C   story
    D   belief
    E   values

17 Another word for 'assiduously' (line 55) could be . . .

    A   meticulously

    B   overtly

    C   unsurprisingly

    D   hastily

    E   lethargically

Now answer these questions about what kinds of words are used in the passage.

18 'sadness and disaster were often to visit' (line 53) is an example of . . .

    A   personification

    B   alliteration

    C   simile

    D   onomatopoeia

    E   ellipsis

19 'associate', 'accomplish', 'develop', 'kept' are what part of speech?

    A   conjunction

    B   noun

    C   preposition

    D   adjective

    E   verb

20 'this paved the way' (line 36) is an example of . . .

    A   personification

    B   alliteration

    C   simile

    D   onomatopoeia

    E   metaphor

In the passage below there are some spelling mistakes. On each line there is either one mistake or no mistake. Find the group of words with the mistake in it and mark its letter on your answer sheet. If there is no mistake, mark 'E' on your answer sheet.

The Robot

21. In a lonely cavern / with dim / lighting, a / metalic form / None
    A / B / C / D / E

22. creaked / into life. Wires like / tenticles spread / all about its / None
    A / B / C / D / E

23. robust limbs, / sending electronic / messages from / the main / None
    A / B / C / D / E

24. proccesing unit / to all the / joints, hydraulic / systems and / None
    A / B / C / D / E

25. motors. Slowly, / delibarately it / stood up on / unsteady feet, / None
    A / B / C / D / E

26. then jerked its / head from left / to right / in an atempt to / None
    A / B / C / D / E

27. identify its / surroundings. / It paused. There / was nothing / None
    A / B / C / D / E

28. familier; / nothing it recognised. / It checked / its internal / None
    A / B / C / D / E

29. messages but / its comanders / had left no / orders or indeed / None
    A / B / C / D / E

30. instructions / of any type. / Its eyes flickered / as it shut / None
    A / B / C / down to wait once more. / E
    D

In the passage below there are some punctuation mistakes. On each line there is either one mistake or no mistake. Find the group of words with the mistake in it and mark its letter on your answer sheet. If there is no mistake, mark 'E' on your answer sheet.

Avalanche!

31. Greta and franz / stared at / the drop which / lay before them. / None
    A / B / C / D / E

32. 'What do you think', / breathed Greta / to her friend. / He was / None
    A / B / C / D / E

33. silent for a moment, / then he turned / to her with / a broad grin / None
    A / B / C / D / E

34. on his face / 'Well there's / only one way / to find out.' With / None
    A / B / C / D / E

35. that, he shrugged / his shoulders, / pulled on / his goggles, and / None
    A / B / C / D / E

36. pushed himself / off the slope. / With only / a moments / None
    A / B / C / D / E

37. hesitation Greta / raced after him, / her ski's gliding / across / None
    A / B / C / D / E

38. the fresh snow / which looked like / icing on a cake. / As they / None
    A / B / C / D / E

39. sped down / the mountain, / a sound like thunder / began to / None
    A / B / C / D / E

40. rumble behind them. / 'Its an / avalanche!' / yelled Greta. / None
    A / B / C / D / E

In each of the questions below you have to choose the best word or group of words to complete the passage so that it makes sense and uses correct, standard English. Choose one of the five answers each time and mark its letter on the answer sheet.

Making Movies

41 There was great | exitment (A) | excitment (B) | excittement (C) | excitement (D) | excited (E) |

42 on the film set. People | scared (A) | scurryed (B) | scurried (C) | scurry (D) | scarred (E) |

43 to and fro | obeying (A) | obaying (B) | obeyed (C) | obey (D) | obayed (E) | instructions and

44 setting up | ekwipment (A) | echwipment (B) | equip (C) | eqipment (D) | equipment (E) |.

45 | Finally (A) | Final (B) | Event (C) | After (D) | Even (E) | everything was ready the director

46 called for | actors (A) | actresses (B) | members (C) | people (D) | producers (E) | of the cast to

47 get ready for the next | seen (A) | scene (B) | film (C) | movie (D) | act (E) |. A blanket of

48 | wool (A) | quite (B) | silents (C) | silence (D) | quietly (E) | descended as the stars of the film

49 entered. Everyone stared in | ore (A) | or (B) | awe (C) | amazing (D) | awesome (E) | at them

50 as they looked so | elegance (A) | elegantly (B) | illegal (C) | eligible (D) | elegant (E) |

ENO OF TEST - PLEASE CHECK ALL YOUR ANSWERS

PRACTISE & PASS 11+

ENGLISH
MULTIPLE CHOICE

PRACTICE PAPER 4

Read the following instructions carefully.

1. Do <u>not</u> begin until you are told to do so.
2. This is a multiple choice test.
3. Answers should be marked on the answer sheet provided.
4. Mark your answer in the same number on the answer sheet as the test question by drawing a firm line clearly through the rectangle next to your answer.
5. If you make a mistake, make sure you rub it out completely before putting a new answer in. There should be only one answer marked for each question.
6. You may do any working out on a separate sheet of paper.
7. Make sure you keep your place on the answer sheet.
8. You will have 50 minutes to complete this test.
9. Work quickly and carefully. If you cannot do a question, do not waste time on it but move on to the next. If you are unsure of the answer, choose the one that you think is best.

Read the passage below carefully and answer the questions that follow.

Maximum Velocity – by P.J. Williams

With a rhythmic whirring, not unlike that of an electric fan on a hot summer's day, the wheels cruise seamlessly past, with powerful pistons pumping in unison as they complete circuit after circuit. It is the definition of poetry in motion. It is a group of athletes cycling around a velodrome in team formation, working together like Canada geese during migration.

5   The group begins at a steady pace – if there can be such a thing in this highly polished wooden arena. Starting low down, the four riders begin to gather speed, following precisely behind one another to prevent loss of speed through air resistance. Then, in a carefully rehearsed move, the lead rider climbs the steep bank at either end of the track, allowing his or her team-mates to hurtle past on the inside lane. When the team has safely passed, the lead rider descends and drops in
10 behind, becoming the last rider. The theory behind this is that each rider takes a turn at the front of the group, setting the pace but having to work harder since the air resistance is stronger here than elsewhere. Then each rider gets to rest behind his or her team-mates while someone else does the hard graft at the front.

The result is a mesmerising display of teamwork carried out at a tremendous pace. And this is
15 just training! During actual races riders can reach breathtaking speeds, using the steep banking to increase their pace. It is testament to the success of the British athletes that in the London Olympics of 2012 there were only 10 events – five each for men and women, with only one rider permitted from each country in the single events. Some claim that this was an attempt to end the dominance of the British athletes who won so many medals at the Beijing Games four
20 years earlier.

But what of the track? Standing at the steepest point and looking down, the 42.5° angle of the London Olympic Velodrome looks almost like a sheer drop. Quite how a cyclist can get a bike to balance on this at speed is hard to imagine, let alone when performing the tactical dance which occurs seemingly in slow motion for such events as the Individual Sprint. The track is
25 constructed from timber – the one in London from Siberian pine – and consists of many strips, pieced together like a Roman mosaic. This is not your average flooring though. Each strip has to be perfectly fitted with those surrounding it: the result is a highly polished surface, tailor-made for speed. At the London Olympic Velodrome racers reached speeds approaching 75 kilometres per hour!

30 The events are different in nature too, and all require a slightly different approach in order to be successful. Some require small groups to work together as a team, some are for individuals and others begin as a large group or peloton with the emphasis on individual success.

The individual sprint

In this event, two riders race against each other. You may be forgiven for thinking that this race seems somewhat bizarre as the two riders start at a strategically slow pace. Sometimes it even looks as though the cyclists have stopped. This can occur for the first two laps then eventually one rider will make a break for it and the other will aim to sit in the slipstream before attempting a passing manoeuvre towards the end of the final lap.

The team sprint

In this event, two teams of three riders begin on opposite sides of the track. The tactics are different as they may be on the same track at the same time but are they not right next to each other. At the end of every lap, each team loses its last rider until there is only one remaining from both teams. The winner is the one to cross their finish line first. The tactics are different in that each team needs to use the slipstream effectively so that the rider at the back gets the most benefit from it before being launched into the final lap.

The keirin

There is no event quite like this as the six riders on the track follow a derny (a small motorcycle), which leads the athletes around the track. It begins slowly but increases its pace as each lap passes then leaves the track altogether with around 700 metres left to go. The cyclists are permitted to jostle for position throughout as long as they remain behind the rear wheel of the motorcycle. Clearly tactics need to be adapted through this race, which often has collisions between cyclists as they fight for advantage on the track.

The keirin was first invented in Japan in 1948, where it is exceptionally popular to this day. It was first contested in the Olympics in 2000.

The team pursuit

The team pursuit consists of two teams of four but this time only the first three cyclists to cross the line count towards the team time. Once again, tactics involve a lot of teamwork, as use of the slipstream and positioning of the riders is paramount to success. Sharing the workload is also important and the lead rider will often be seen climbing high onto the bank to allow his or her team-mates through, joining them at the back of the group. These pursuit races can be incredibly close and, in a similar way to the individual pursuit, teams finish their race and record their time at the same place they began.

The omnium

This was a new event for the 2012 Olympics in London, although it really consists of several events. It has been dubbed the decathlon of the cycling events although it has only six races over

Go straight on to the next page

two days and not ten. The winner of each of the races scores one point, second place scores two points and so on. After the two days of races, the overall winner is the cyclist with the lowest number of points. The races are:

1. a 250m lap against the clock
2. an elimination race – the rider in last place every two laps is eliminated until there is only one remaining
3. an individual pursuit
4. a 1km time trial (500m for women)
5. a points race – this is a bit more complicated as points are awarded periodically throughout the race for sprints and if the field is lapped. It is a much longer race so good endurance is vital
6. a scratch race which is similar to the points race except it doesn't have points!

In addition to the variety of races and events, there are also some specific terms that spectators would do well to remember. The word *repechage*, which also appears in other sports such as rowing, means that a particular team or contestant has a second chance having lost a previous heat. Should they win the *repechage*, they proceed through to the next round.

The word 'slipstream' describes what happens when a cyclist follows another very closely. It is a word that is also often used in motor sports. It means that the lead rider makes a hole in the air as they travel around the track; any rider following closely will have less air resistance to cycle against, so will have an easier journey around the track. Therefore, getting in someone's slipstream can be very advantageous.

Without doubt, cycling has increased in popularity in recent years. Judging by the excitement it delivers this is no great surprise. It offers tactics, endurance and explosive power in a variety of events for both men and women.

Now answer these questions (look at the passage again if you need to). You should choose the best answer and mark its letter on your answer sheet.

1 In which race would you see a small motorcycle?

- A   individual pursuit
- B   team pursuit
- C   scratch race
- D   elimination race
- E   keirin

2 Why does the lead rider in a team allow their team-mates to ride past after each lap?

- A   to share the workload
- B   because their team-mates are faster
- C   because their team-mates will complain otherwise
- D   because they are too tired to continue
- E   to have a break for a drink

3 Why will riders sometimes ride high on the banking?

- A   to get a better view
- B   to make space for other riders
- C   to use it to increase their speed
- D   to freewheel down for a rest
- E   to avoid collisions

4 Why does the author describe the London track as 'tailor-made for speed'?

- A   The track was constructed extremely quickly.
- B   Only the fastest riders are allowed on the track.
- C   The track was made from pieces of Siberian pine.
- D   The track was made specifically so riders will go faster.
- E   The track has a 42.5° angled banking at each end.

5 What is the name given to the heat for those cyclists who have lost a previous heat?

- A keirin
- B slipstream
- C elimination
- D derny
- E *repechage*

6 What is the main advantage of sitting in someone's slipstream?

- A It allows the cyclist to go faster.
- B It allows the cyclist to conserve energy.
- C It makes it harder for other cyclists to get past.
- D It makes it harder for the lead cyclist to see where the others are.
- E It helps prevent collisions.

7 In which event are cyclists likely to go slowest at the start?

- A keirin
- B elimination
- C team sprint
- D omnium
- E individual sprint

8 Why do you think the omnium has been dubbed the decathlon of cycling events?

- A It lasts for more than one day.
- B It is really difficult to win.
- C It has the same scoring system as the decathlon.
- D It has lots of events like the decathlon.
- E It takes place on a track like the decathlon.

Go straight on to the next page

9 Who is likely to take part in a *repechage*?

A a trainer
B the winner of a heat
C the loser of a heat
D a pursuit team
E a participant in the omnium

10 How many riders need to cross the line for the final lap of a team pursuit?

A 1
B 2
C 3
D 4
E all of them

11 Which statement is not correct for the elimination race in the omnium?

A Always try to stay near the front.
B Always try to stay ahead of someone.
C Make sure you are not last every two laps.
D It doesn't matter where you are as long as you do well on the final lap of the race.
E The winner of the race gets one point.

12 In which country was the keirin first used?

A London
B Japan
C Britain
D America
E Australia

13 Why do you think the designers of the London track hoped that it would help the cyclists achieve high speeds?

   A   It would make crashes more likely.
   B   It would make the riders look faster.
   C   It would help break world records in events.
   D   It would get the events done more quickly.
   E   It would help the athletes win more medals.

Now answer these questions about the meanings of words and how they are used in the passage.

14 The 'peloton' (line 32) refers to . . .

   A   individual cyclists
   B   a group of cyclists
   C   a cycling arena
   D   a group working together
   E   the races for cyclists

15 'carefully rehearsed' (line 7) means . . .

   A   well practised
   B   cycling rapidly
   C   repeatedly
   D   never tried before
   E   brand new

16 Another word for 'paramount' (line 54) could be . . .

   A   key
   B   largest
   C   most reliable
   D   inevitable
   E   tantamount

17 Another word for 'manoeuvre' (line 37) could be . . .

    A   accelerate
    B   sprint
    C   strategy
    D   movement
    E   decision

Now answer these questions about what kinds of words are used in the passage.

18 'like a Roman mosaic' (line 26) is an example of . . .

    A   personification
    B   alliteration
    C   simile
    D   onomatopoeia
    E   metaphor

19 'powerful pistons pumping' (line 2) is what part of speech?

    A   personification
    B   alliteration
    C   simile
    D   onomatopoeia
    E   metaphor

20 'tactics', 'endurance', 'doubt', 'excitement' are what type of word?

    A   collective noun
    B   concrete noun
    C   proper noun
    D   abstract noun
    E   pronoun

Go straight on to the next page

In the passage below there are some spelling mistakes. On each line there is either one mistake or no mistake. Find the group of words with the mistake in it and mark its letter on your answer sheet. If there is no mistake, mark 'E' on your answer sheet.

The Disc Jockey

21. TJ works as a | pressenter | on the radio. | Every morning | he — None
　　　　　A　　　　　　B　　　　　　　C　　　　　　　D　　　　E

22. wakes up | whiles | the sky is still dark | and makes | his way — None
　　　　A　　　B　　　　　C　　　　　　　　D　　　　E

23. into the studio. | First | he collects | his playlist | which tells — None
　　　　A　　　　　B　　　C　　　　　D　　　　　E

24. him the names | of the songs | to play each | our. | Next he — None
　　　　A　　　　　B　　　　　C　　　　D　　　E

25. swiches | on the news | and gathers | the latest headlines | to — None
　　　A　　　　B　　　　　C　　　　　D　　　　E

26. let his | liseners | know | what is going on | in the world. And — None
　　　A　　　B　　　C　　　　D　　　　　E

27. finally | he settles himself | into his chair | and puts | his — None
　　　A　　　　B　　　　　C　　　　D　　　E

28. headphones on. | Then he waits | for his | producor's | signal — None
　　　　A　　　　　B　　　　　C　　　D　　　　E

29. before | comencing | his show. | It's called | *Breakfast with TJ* — None
　　　A　　　B　　　　C　　　　D　　　E

30. and is | extremely | popular | with the local | comunity. — None
　　　A　　　B　　　　C　　　D　　　　E

48　　Go straight on to the next page

In the passage below there are some punctuation mistakes. On each line there is either one mistake or no mistake. Find the group of words with the mistake in it and mark its letter on your answer sheet. If there is no mistake, mark 'E' on your answer sheet.

The Departure Lounge

31. Adi, and his family strolled through the airport with their / None
    A   B   C   D   E

32. cases stacked upon a metal trolley. Adis brother Marlon / None
    A   B   C   D   E

33. stared at everything, and his parent's had to keep telling / None
    A   B   C   D   E

34. him to keep up with them. 'but it's so interesting,' Marlon / None
    A   B   C   D   E

35. explained as his father chivvied him along one more time / None
    A   B   C   D   E

36. His mother smiled at him 'Are you excited about our trip?' / None
    A   B   C   D   E

37. she asked. 'Of course! It's going to be fabulous' he / None
    A   B   C   D   E

38. gushed. 'Come on Marlon,' said Adi. 'Let me take that / None
    A   B   C   D   E

39. bag for you, then you can have a good look at everything. / None
    A   B   C   D   E

40. Marlon beamed at his brother as they walked to the plane / None
    A   B   C   D   E

In each of the questions below you have to choose the best word or group of words to complete the passage so that it makes sense and uses correct, standard English. Choose one of the five answers each time and mark its letter on the answer sheet.

An Electric Journey

41 Standing gleaming in the [station A] [platform B] [track C] [rails D] [kiosk E] the

42 train [expands A] [exacts B] [extent C] [extends D] [expires E] for fully twenty

43 carriages. Each [curtails A] [contents B] [contains C] [certain D] [curtains E] many

44 [amiable A] [compromising B] [comfort C] [affable D] [comfortable E] seats and also

45 [species A] [spacious B] [spatial C] [special D] [spartan E] tables on which people can

46 work. As the train [glades A] [glides B] [gleans C] [glows D] [glistens E] out of the

47 station the passengers look [forward A] [backward B] [forth C] [around D] [about E]

48 to a smooth and [elating A] [relating B] [relapsing C] [relaxing D] [reliving E] ride.

49 The high speed [electrocute A] [elected B] [electronic C] [elastic D] [electric E]

50 train [transponds A] [tracks B] [trajects C] [transports D] [tramples E] its passengers safely to their destination.

PRACTISE AND PASS 11+
WRITING

Read the following instructions carefully.

1. Do <u>not</u> begin until you are told to do so.
2. You may make rough plans on a separate piece of paper but do not take too long to do so as time is limited.
3. If you fill the writing paper provided you may continue on another piece of lined paper.
4. Try to make your writing as interesting as possible and ensure that your sentences are structured correctly. Make sure that your handwriting is neat.
5. You will have 30 minutes to complete your written work.

TITLE 1

Use the title below and write a story about it. Try to make your story as interesting as possible.

An Exciting Journey

TITLE 2

Using the question below write a short essay to explain what you would do to solve this problem.

<u>How can children be encouraged to read more?</u>

TITLE 3

Use the title below and write a story about it. Try to make your story as interesting as possible.

<u>The Flood!</u>

TITLE 4

Use the sentence below as the beginning of a story. You need to write the middle and end of the story.

<u>The two children heard heavy footsteps approaching. Looking about wildly for somewhere to hide, all they could think was, 'We shouldn't be here.'</u>

TITLE 5

Using the statement below write a short essay explaining how we can achieve this goal. How could this aim make the world a better place?

We should all try to help those who need it whenever we can.

TITLE 6

Use the title below and write a story about it. Try to make your story as interesting as possible.

An Undiscovered World

TITLE 7

Use the sentence below as the beginning of a story. You need to write the middle and end of the story.

<u>A low rumbling sound began as the enormous boulder rolled away from the mountain. When it stopped and the dust settled, the adventurers could see the entrance to a deep cavern.</u>

TITLE 8

Use the title below and write a story about it. Try to make your story as interesting as possible.

<u>A Wonderful Invention</u>

_____
_____
_____
_____
_____
_____
_____
_____
_____
_____
_____
_____
_____
_____
_____

PRACTISE & PASS 11+

ENGLISH
ANSWER GRIDS

Students should mark their answers to the practice papers in this answer booklet

Contents

Practice paper 1	3
Practice paper 2	4
Practice paper 3	5
Practice paper 4	6

© Peter Williams and Trotman Publishing, 2015

The right of Peter Williams to be identified as the author of this work has been asserted by him in accordance with the Copyright, Designs and Patents Act, 1988.

All rights reserved. No part of this publication may be transmitted in any form or by any means, or stored in a retrieval system without prior written permission from the publisher.

First published 2015 by Trotman Publishing, a division of Crimson Publishing Ltd, 19–21c Charles Street, Bath BA1 1HX.

ISBN 978 1 84455 427 0

A catalogue record for this book is available from the British Library.

PRACTICE PAPER 1

Student's name

School name

Date of test

Please mark answers like this ▭

Waterways of the World

The Police Report

In the Mountains

A Difficult Voyage

PRACTICE PAPER 2

Student's name

School name

Date of test

Please mark answers like this ▭

Behind the Bookcase

A Cold-Blooded Life

At the Market

In the Moonlight

PRACTICE PAPER 3

Student's name

School name

Date of test

Please mark answers like this ▭

A Remarkable Scientist

The Robot

Avalanche!

Making Movies

PRACTICE PAPER 4

Student's name

School name

Date of test

Please mark answers like this ▭

Maximum Velocity

The Disc Jockey

The Departure Lounge

An Electric Journey

PRACTISE & PASS 11+

ENGLISH
ANSWERS AND ADVICE FOR PARENTS

Read this <u>before</u> the student starts taking any of the practice test papers.

Contents

⚙ Timings and rules for English practice papers	2
⚙ Suggested mock test schedule	2
⚙ Marking the tests: correct answers and answer explanations	4
Practice paper 1	4
Practice paper 2	6
Practice paper 3	8
Practice paper 4	10
⚙ How to improve scores	12
⚙ Advice on marking the writing paper	14

© Peter Williams and Trotman Publishing, 2015

The right of Peter Williams to be identified as the author of this work has been asserted by him in accordance with the Copyright, Designs and Patents Act, 1988.

All rights reserved. No part of this publication may be transmitted in any form or by any means, or stored in a retrieval system without prior written permission from the publisher.

First published 2015 by Trotman Publishing, a division of Crimson Publishing Ltd, 19–21c Charles Street, Bath BA1 1HX.

ISBN 978 1 84455 427 0

A catalogue record for this book is available from the British Library.

TIMINGS AND RULES FOR ENGLISH PRACTICE PAPERS

SETTING THE TEST

- Students should be allowed 50 minutes to complete each English paper.
- The students are expected to read all of the instructions and passages themselves within the 50 minutes.
- Do not read or explain any words to the student.
- A dictionary or thesaurus may **not** be used.
- Time the test precisely and stop the student when the allotted time is over.
- Students may be informed when they are halfway through the allotted time and when there are five minutes remaining.

GUIDANCE FOR TESTING

- Do explain to students before the test that there will be some very difficult questions and they could appear at any point in the test. Tell students to mark these on the paper and come back to them. Tell them not to waste time fretting about really tough questions, just to get on and answer those questions they know how to!
- Get students to check they have marked an answer in each answer grid – often students forget to do this for each question or mark them in the wrong order or even mark two on one grid and none on the next.

SUGGESTED MOCK TEST SCHEDULE

If you want the student to take the practice papers in a mock test format, then you can follow the suggestions below on how to do this. All exams are different in nature so the order in which papers are given and which question styles are included can vary. If the student has worked through *Practise & Pass 11+ Level One: Discover English* and *Practise & Pass 11+ Level Two: Develop English* they will be familiar with the most common question styles.

SET UP

- Set up a clear desk. Have a pencil, rubber and spare blank paper set out.
- Make sure a simple, analogue clock is easily visible.
- Follow all rules and timings precisely (see above).
- Do not give any extra help even if you can see that the student is making a mistake.
- If the student requires a bathroom break during a paper, let them but explain that no extra time will be given.
- Try to get the student to use the full amount of time – they will not be allowed to leave the room early in the actual exam.

WRITING PAPER

If you want to set the writing paper as part of your mock test choose just one title for your child to do. Do not give them a choice of titles unless the school for which you are preparing specifically does this. If you decide to give your child more than one set of mock exams, try choosing a different type of writing title so that they have experience of creative writing and non-fiction styles.

Note: Different schools allocate different time limits for the writing paper (if they are setting one), from 20 minutes to 45 minutes. You should check with the school how much time will be allowed but if no time is given, or you are unable to find out, allow the student 30 minutes to sit the writing paper.

INCLUDING OTHER TESTS

If you want to replicate a true exam experience, give the student other test types to do, using the other titles in the *Practise & Pass 11+ Level Three* series. Follow the suggested times given for each type of test and give the student a 10 minute break to have a quick drink and use the bathroom after completing each test.

Note: It is rare for students to have to take papers in all areas so it is important for parents to find out which papers are relevant and have the student take only those.

Once you know which papers your child needs to sit then set out a schedule as follows.

- Test 1: 50 minutes
- Break: 10 minutes
- Test 2: 50 minutes
- Break: 10 minutes
- Test 3: 50 minutes

Please note that non-verbal reasoning has different timings to English, maths and verbal reasoning so take account of this when planning your 'mock' day for your child.

MARKING THE TESTS: CORRECT ANSWERS AND ANSWER EXPLANATIONS

The following pages contain the correct answers for Practice Papers 1, 2, 3 and 4. If a student has answered incorrectly go through the question with them to ensure they understand where they went wrong. If they are still struggling go back to the relevant sections of *Practise & Pass 11+ Level One: Discover English* and *Practise & Pass 11+ Level Two: Develop English* and practise those types of question again. You can also refer to the section on how to improve scores (p. 12) for tips on further practice.

When marking the tests remember there are no half marks – the answer should be marked as either correct or incorrect. Any workings out on scrap paper should not be marked. If the student has written the correct answer on a piece of working out paper but marked the incorrect letter on the corresponding grid answer sheet, the answer is incorrect.

It is vital that students practise how to mark the correct answer on the multiple choice grids so do not consider any working out on scrap paper.

PRACTICE PAPER 1

Question	Answer
1.	D: Suez Canal
2.	E: Red Sea and Mediterranean Sea
3.	C: Because the two seas it linked were at different heights.
4.	C: The Suez Canal is older and larger than the Panama Canal.
5.	A: They had to get rid of swarms of mosquitoes.
6.	A: 0
7.	D: It has only one lane for ships with passing points.
8.	B: The railways had become too expensive.
9.	A: It significantly reduced the distance ships had to travel.
10.	B: Charles V of Spain commissioned architects to look into it.
11.	E: 7 to 8 hours
12.	C: It is able to raise and lower huge ships using several locks.
13.	C: Global man-made water links
14.	E: a narrow strip of land between two seas
15.	B: dug out
16.	B: ship
17.	E: negotiate
18.	B: alliteration
19.	D: adjective
20.	D: abstract noun

Question	Answer
21.	C: and gloomey (should be gloomy)
22.	A: at the sceen (should be scene)
23.	E: None
24.	D: As I was preceeding (should be proceeding)
25.	A: in a westerley (should be westerly)
26.	C: which dissapeared (should be disappeared)
27.	D: suspitious so that (should be suspicious)
28.	E: None
29.	B: my colleages (should be colleagues)
30.	A: to apprahend (should be apprehend)
31.	C: friend penny as (should be Penny)
32.	C: ledge Using (should have a full stop after ledge)
33.	A: placed handhold's, (handholds, no apostrophe)
34.	E: None
35.	D: amazing view? (should be a full stop not a question mark)
36.	A: 'Isnt it (should be Isn't with an apostrophe)
37.	B: Awesome,' replied (should be a speech mark before the word Awesome)
38.	B: forests, rivers, (don't need a comma after rivers before and)
39.	D: even higher? (missing closing speech mark)
40.	E: None
41.	B: pitched
42.	D: fury
43.	B: tropical
44.	A: passengers
45.	E: hull
46.	E: creaked
47.	D: crashed
48.	B: vessel
49.	A: abated
50.	C: travellers

PRACTICE PAPER 2

Question	Answer
1.	C: It was a safe place to be alone.
2.	C: a watcher
3.	E: She injected poison when she bit.
4.	A: different sized books
5.	D: She noticed a shadow moving on the wall.
6.	E: a secret room
7.	B: under the floorboards
8.	C: She could hurt them with her venomous bite.
9.	C: She and Octavia do not meet any more.
10.	E: Those books had not been read for a long time.
11.	B: Because they are slower and have to get close before they attack.
12.	C: a hand
13.	C: She resents the fact that as Octavia is not poisonous she is not hunted.
14.	C: a place of safety
15.	B: The shadow on the wall warned of danger.
16.	D: peculiarly
17.	E: randomly
18.	C: simile
19.	B: noun
20.	D: onomatopoeia
21.	D: have sufered the (should be suffered)
22.	A: unenvyable fate (should be unenviable)
23.	E: None
24.	D: is sumwhat (should be somewhat)
25.	C: fasinating animals (should be fascinating)
26.	A: inturnal way (should be internal)
27.	D: would explaine (should be explain)
28.	E: None
29.	B: Durring daylight (should be During)
30.	C: become preditors (should be predators)

Question	Answer
31.	A: The traders' (should be traders, no apostrophe)
32.	D: clive ran the fruit (should be Clive with a capital C)
33.	C: good friend's, (should be friends, no apostrophe)
34.	E: None
35.	A: 'How's your foot' (needs a question mark after foot)
36.	B: wares one day (needs a full stop after day)
37.	A: better, responded (missing closing speech mark after better,)
38.	C: asked Amir. 'i (should be I)
39.	E: None
40.	D: be better soon' (needs a full stop after soon)
41.	D: galleon
42.	B: sheltered
43.	B: sails
44.	E: deck
45.	A: barked
46.	B: weigh
47.	C: aboard
48.	D: heaved
49.	C: jetty
50.	B: contraband

PRACTICE PAPER 3

Question	Answer
1.	D: a radiologist
2.	C: Polish
3.	D: 1911
4.	E: She wanted all scientists to be able to use her knowledge.
5.	D: She convinced the French government to set up a Radium Institute.
6.	B: the First World War
7.	B: Her mother and sister died while she was still at school.
8.	A: Her husband had been killed in an accident.
9.	D: She knew it was important but longed to be conducting research.
10.	B: It was caused by being too close to radium.
11.	D: She was unaware of the dangers of radiation.
12.	C: pieces of metal
13.	A: They felt with their hands and watched how their patients responded.
14.	A: moved by hand
15.	D: Her ideas were very advanced for the time in which she lived.
16.	A: heritage
17.	A: meticulously
18.	A: personification
19.	E: verb
20.	E: metaphor
21.	D: a metalic form (should be metallic)
22.	B: Wires like tenticles (should be tentacles)
23.	E: None
24.	A: proccesing unit (should be processing)
25.	B: delibarately it (should be deliberately)
26.	D: in an atempt to (should be attempt)
27.	E: None
28.	A: familier; nothing (should be familiar)
29.	B: its comanders (should be commanders)
30.	E: None

Question	Answer
31.	A: Greta and franz (should be Franz with a capital)
32.	B: think', breathed (should have a question mark after think)
33.	E: None
34.	A: on his face (missing full stop or comma after face)
35.	D: goggles, and (don't need a comma before and)
36.	D: a moments (should be moment's with an apostrophe)
37.	C: her ski's (skis shouldn't have an apostrophe)
38.	E: None
39.	E: None
40.	B: them. 'Its (should be 'It's)
41.	D: excitement
42.	C: scurried
43.	A: obeying
44.	E: equipment
45.	D: After
46.	C: members
47.	B: scene
48.	D: silence
49.	C: awe
50.	E: elegant

PRACTICE PAPER 4

Question	Answer
1.	E: keirin
2.	A: to share the workload
3.	C: to use it to increase their speed
4.	D: The track was made specifically so riders will go faster.
5.	E: *repechage*
6.	B: It allows the cyclist to conserve energy.
7.	E: individual sprint
8.	D: It has lots of events like the decathlon.
9.	C: the loser of a heat
10.	C: 3
11.	D: It doesn't matter where you are as long as you do well on the final lap of the race.
12.	B: Japan
13.	C: It would help break world records in events.
14.	B: a group of cyclists
15.	A: well practised
16.	A: key
17.	D: movement
18.	C: simile
19.	B: alliteration
20.	D: abstract noun
21.	B: a pressenter on (should be presenter)
22.	A: wakes up whiles (should be while)
23.	E: None
24.	D: our. Next he (should be hour)
25.	A: swiches on the (should be switches)
26.	A: let his liseners (should be listeners)
27.	E: None
28.	D: producor's signal (should be producer)
29.	A: before comencing (should be commencing)
30.	D: comunity. (should be community)

Question	Answer
31.	A: Adi, and his (doesn't need a comma after Adi)
32.	C: trolley. Adis (should be Adi's)
33.	C: parent's had (should be parents, without an apostrophe)
34.	C: 'but it's so (should be But with a capital B)
35.	D: one more time (should have a full stop after time)
36.	B: smiled at him (should have a full stop after him)
37.	D: fabulous' he (needs a comma after fabulous)
38.	E: None
39.	D: look at everything. (needs speech mark after everything.)
40.	D: to the plane (needs a full stop after plane)
41.	A: station
42.	D: extends
43.	C: contains
44.	E: comfortable
45.	B: spacious
46.	B: glides
47.	A: forward
48.	D: relaxing
49.	E: electric
50.	D: transports

HOW TO IMPROVE SCORES

Students scoring 7 out of 10 or less for spelling, punctuation and grammar may require further practice. There are several ways students can improve upon their initial scores. Here are some more hints and tips to help them achieve a better score.

TIMINGS

Often students either struggle to complete all the questions in the time, or they race through and finish with a lot of time to spare. Neither of these situations is ideal.

If your child was not able to finish all of the questions you need to find out why. Ask them to point out any difficult questions which they encountered in the paper and this will be where they have lost time. Encourage them to practise these questions but also encourage them to 'skip' these questions, complete the paper and then return to them at the end. In this way your child will get to see all of the questions and spend enough time on those questions they find easier before tackling the more difficult ones.

If your child is a fast worker, you need to try and slow them down a little. The main reason for this is that you don't want them misreading questions because they are going too fast. Encourage them to underline key words in questions and to look at the examples – where given – so they really understand what to do. The more they make notes and write things down, the less likely they are to miss vital information.

FURTHER TIPS

- Do tell students to write down workings for each question where possible. These will prove invaluable when checking at the end. This can be particularly helpful when trying to spot spelling mistakes or punctuation errors. Writing a word down with several different spellings often helps us decide if it 'looks' right, for example.
- Get students to check they have marked an answer in each answer grid – often students forget to do this for each question or mark them in the wrong order or even mark two on one grid and none on the next.

FURTHER PRACTICE

It's well worth going over any questions your child got wrong and explaining to them how to get the right answer. If you'd like more questions of a certain type to practise or if you're unsure of the best way to explain a particular question, use the following breakdown of where to find different question types in the first two titles in the Practise & Pass series, *Practise & Pass 11+ Level One: Discover English* and *Practise & Pass 11+ Level Two: Develop English*. That way you can find out how best to explain the questions to them and also give your child lots more practice to help them improve.

Practice paper 1

Question	Type	*Practise & Pass 11+ Level One: Discover English* lessons to refer to for further practice	*Practise & Pass 11+ Level Two: Develop English* lessons to refer to for further practice
1–20	Comprehension, parts of speech, vocabulary	Lessons 4, 8, 12, 16	Lessons 4, 8, 12, 16 – A, B and Practice
21–30	Spelling	Lessons 1, 5, 9, 13	Lessons 1, 5, 9, 13
31–40	Punctuation	Lessons 3, 7, 11, 15	Lessons 3, 7, 11, 15
41–50	Sentence structure	Lessons 2, 6, 10, 14	Lessons 2, 6, 10, 14

Practice paper 2

Question	Type	*Practise & Pass 11+ Level One: Discover English* lessons to refer to for further practice	*Practise & Pass 11+ Level Two: Develop English* lessons to refer to for further practice
1–20	Comprehension, parts of speech, vocabulary	Lessons 4, 8, 12, 16	Lessons 4, 8, 12, 16 – A, B and Practice
21–30	Spelling	Lessons 1, 5, 9, 13	Lessons 1, 5, 9, 13
31–40	Punctuation	Lessons 3, 7, 11, 15	Lessons 3, 7, 11, 15
41–50	Sentence structure	Lessons 2, 6, 10, 14	Lessons 2, 6, 10, 14

Practice paper 3

Question	Type	*Practise & Pass 11+ Level One: Discover English* lessons to refer to for further practice	*Practise & Pass 11+ Level Two: Develop English* lessons to refer to for further practice
1–20	Comprehension, parts of speech, vocabulary	Lessons 4, 8, 12, 16	Lessons 4, 8, 12, 16 – A, B and Practice
21–30	Spelling	Lessons 1, 5, 9, 13	Lessons 1, 5, 9, 13
31–40	Punctuation	Lessons 3, 7, 11, 15	Lessons 3, 7, 11, 15
41–50	Sentence structure	Lessons 2, 6, 10, 14	Lessons 2, 6, 10, 14

Practice paper 4

Question	Type	*Practise & Pass 11+ Level One: Discover English* lessons to refer to for further practice	*Practise & Pass 11+ Level Two: Develop English* lessons to refer to for further practice
1–20	Comprehension, parts of speech, vocabulary	Lessons 4, 8, 12, 16	Lessons 4, 8, 12, 16 – A, B and Practice
21–30	Spelling	Lessons 1, 5, 9, 13	Lessons 1, 5, 9, 13
31–40	Punctuation	Lessons 3, 7, 11, 15	Lessons 3, 7, 11, 15
41–50	Sentence structure	Lessons 2, 6, 10, 14	Lessons 2, 6, 10, 14

ADVICE ON MARKING THE WRITING PAPER

The writing paper is exceptionally difficult to mark since everyone can have a different opinion as to what makes a good piece of writing. Many schools use the writing element of a test as a tie-breaker; that is, if a student has not quite reached the pass mark but comes close the school might assess the writing task. If the writing is deemed to be of a good standard this can put the student's result up to the 'pass after review' group, so it is worth practising. Some schools use writing as part of their English paper so you should find out if this is true for your child. Students may be presented with a creative writing title (asking them to write a story) or a non-fiction title (asking them to write an essay explaining their opinion or view) so make sure they are prepared for both.

All schools will have their own marking criteria so it is impossible to give a precise marking guide. However, listed below is a checklist of things to look out for. After the student has completed the writing task, give them a copy of this checklist and ask them to tick all of the elements they think they have included. Sit down and discuss the checklist with them, pointing out any elements which have been used and explaining how other elements could be incorporated.

Lesson 17 in *Practise & Pass 11+ Level Two: Develop English* provides further coaching and advice on the writing paper.

CREATIVE WRITING

Titles 1, 3, 4, 6, 7 and 8 are creative writing titles. Use the checklist below to judge how many elements the student has managed to incorporate.

Creative writing checklist	Check
Does my story follow a sequence of events?	
Have I included one or more characters and have I given sufficient information about them before telling the story?	
Have I included and described an interesting setting?	
Do I have a main plot/story line and does this follow through my story?	
Do I have a plausible ending which fits in with the rest of the story?	
Have I used a variety of verbs, adjectives and conjunctions (sentence connectives)?	
Have I tried to use figurative language – such as similes, metaphors, alliteration and personification – to make my writing more colourful?	
Have I tried to vary the length of my sentences to help create different moods?	
Have I used direct speech for my characters where necessary?	
Have I tried to use simple and more complex sentences to vary my writing?	

Grammar/spelling/punctuation checklist	Check
Have I read through my work to make sure I have not repeated or left out any words in sentences?	
Have I checked all of the basic spelling words that I should know?	
Have I checked all of the basic punctuation such as full stops, capital letters, question marks, apostrophes and speech marks?	
Have I repeated myself too often?	
Have I checked that I have not over-used adjectives and added more words than are necessary?	
Do my subjects and verbs agree?	
Have I used the same tense of verb consistently in my writing?	
Have I read through my work to see if I can improve any of the phrases?	
Have I checked that I have not used slang/non-standard English except where my characters are speaking?	
Is my handwriting legible? (Remember – if you can't read it easily then your teachers won't be able to either!)	

NON-FICTION WRITING

Titles 2 and 5 are non-fiction titles. Use the checklist below to judge how many elements the student has managed to incorporate.

Non-fiction writing checklist	Check
Have I understood the title and written about it?	
Have I used vocabulary to explain my feelings?	
Have I included and described an interesting setting?	
Does my account follow a clear sequence of events?	
Does my ending bring a satisfactory conclusion to my account?	
Have I used a variety of verbs, adjectives and conjunctions (sentence connectives)?	
Have I tried to use figurative language – such as similes, metaphors, alliteration and personification – to make my writing more colourful?	
Have I tried to vary the length of my sentences to help create different moods?	
Have I tried to use simple and more complex sentences to vary my writing?	
Have I used persuasive language and made a logical argument for titles which require this?	
Have I made good use of questions to appeal to the readers' emotions?	

Grammar/spelling/punctuation checklist	Check
Have I read through my work to make sure I have not repeated or left out any words in sentences?	
Have I checked all of the basic spelling words that I should know?	
Have I checked all of the basic punctuation such as full stops, capital letters, question marks, apostrophes and speech marks?	
Have I repeated myself too often?	
Have I checked that I have not over-used adjectives and added more words than are necessary?	
Do my subjects and verbs agree?	
Have I used the same tense of verb consistently in my writing?	
Have I read through my work to see if I can improve any of the phrases?	
Have I checked that I have not used slang/non-standard English?	
Is my handwriting legible? (Remember – if you can't read it easily then your teachers won't be able to either!)	